Looking for Gold!

Written by Gemma Bagnall

Illustrated by Eva Morales

It was Friday afternoon, and Miss Aman couldn't wait to show the children her box of stories.

"But that's just junk!" said Jen, as Miss Aman lifted the lid.

"No, it's not," said Bella-Rose, picking up a plastic tube. "This is going to be a telescope in my story. My grandad tells the best stories – and now I'll tell them too!"

"Perfect," said Miss Aman as her eyes lit up. "Use it over the weekend!"

Bella-Rose, Billy and Tam set sail with the telescope in their pretend boat.

"Shiver me timbers!" Bella-Rose shouted.

Following an old brown map, they went in search of long-lost gold.

"Be careful, shipmates!" called Grandad Steve. "I've seen hungry giant sharks in these waves, and they could snap you up!"

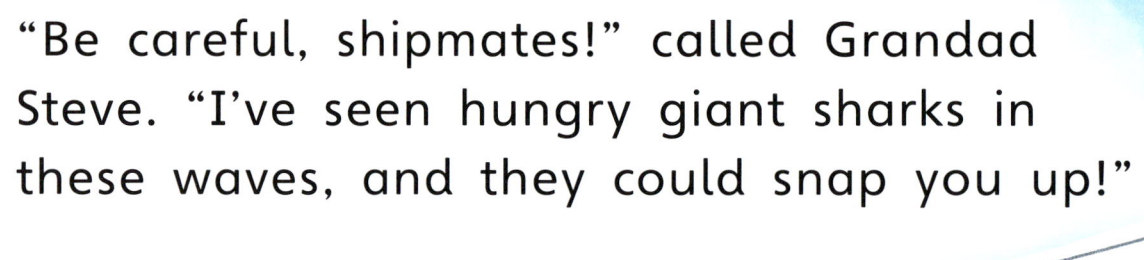

"Never fear – I'll save us!" said Bella-Rose.

"I'm brave and strong. I could fight a hundred sharks!"

"Land ahoy!" shouted Bella-Rose, peering through the telescope. "It's time to get that gold!"

As they left the ship, Tam landed with a splash.

He was stuck!

"Quicksand is no challenge for me!" Billy cried, putting all his energy into pulling Tam out of the thick sludge.

"I think I see the gold," said Bella-Rose, pointing to a cross on the map.

Looking up, they spotted a huge pile of golden leaves under the old oak tree.

"We did it!" they cried as they collected their loot.

They got back to Bella-Rose's trailer just in time for Tam's dad to collect him.

"Look at all the gold we found!" said Tam.

"Where will the box of stories take us next?" asked Bella-Rose.

"I can't wait to find out!" Billy laughed.